CHAAT

CHAAT

Poems by
Emer Davis

THE BROWSER
www.thebrowser.org
Publishers & Booksellers

Title:
Chaat: Poems by Emer Davis

Author's Name:
Emer Davis

First Published in India in 2021 by The Browser
(An imprint of J.G.S. Enterprises Pvt. Ltd.)

Publisher's Address:
SCO 14-15, FF, Sector 8-C, Chandigarh 160 009
Email: service@thebrowser.org

Edition: I

ISBN: 978-81-949542-0-0

Printed in India at Thomson Press (India) Ltd.

THE BROWSER
www.thebrowser.org
Publishers & Booksellers

Dedicated to:

Maura and John, who both encouraged me to write when I was a child, and follow my own path in life.

Better than a thousand hollow words is one word that brings peacc.

—Buddha

Contents

Foreword

All the poems in this collection were written in India, except for the first poem, "The Shopping List", which was written about my impending relocation to Delhi.

It's a collection of my experiences and thoughts while living in India. I decided to call the book "Chaat" which is the Indian equivalent of western fast food. Chaat is street food with fresh ingredients, prepared and served instantly. Diverse street vendors are dotted across every village, town and city in India selling this delicious food.

The English word "chat" means to talk and have a conversation. And this is what my book explores. It's a collection of diverse ramblings I had while living in India. It represents the fusion of life here reverberating from every street corner.

All the poems have been on the Bunnacurry Poet Facebook page, and several of the poems have been previously published online.

Emer Davis

The Shopping List

The shopping list gets longer,
Kerrygold butter
Tayto
Antiseptic wipes
Imodium tablets
Lice combs
Mosquito repellant spray
Calpol
Cases full of a chemical overload,
We think about
what we won't have there,
And forget about
the things that will be there.

When we arrive,
a city polluted in a sensory overload,
A carousel of sights and sounds
bombarding our fragile frames,
An array of colours
that will indulge our souls,
Weeping children begging
for a few rupees,
The incessant noise
of motor engines and voices
reverberating,

A kaleidoscope of people
crashing past our window pane
in rush hour traffic,
These are the things
which are not on our list,
Over packed suitcases
bulging with anticipation,
We try to hold onto what
makes us safe,
Oversized baggage disappearing
on the conveyor belt,
We walk through the departure lounge
and make another list
of all the things we want to see.

The Taj Mahal,
Jaipur,
The Red Fort,
The National Railway Museum in Delhi,
The list gets longer,
A sensory overload
waiting for us to indulge our curiosity,
Our new home beckons
as we travel east.

First Impressions

Lush green trees, verdant and evergreen,
virgin leaves glittering in the monsoon dew,
large drops blurring the window pane,
we drive through wide avenues
in the diplomatic enclave,
green and yellow *tuk-tuks* weaving
in and out of traffic,
the rawness of life stationed at every corner,
taxis and ubers vying for space,
screech to a halt
as an officer raises his hand,
stopping and starting,
unprepared for
the slow crawl and angry fists,
we glimpse snatches of Indian life
played out along the roadside,
a barber gliding a razor over
a foam-lathered face in his mobile stall,
unbeaten souls refusing to go away,
refusing to disappear and be forgotten.

The Tracks

A line drawn in front of me,
old carriages rattle by,
a relic from another time,
I follow the scent left behind,
dingy coaches, battered and bruised,
overloaded with human cargo,
deviated from their route,
empty railcars stalled for hours,
the overnight sleeper cruises by,
under the soft glow of the moon's shadow,
a celestial interlude breaking through,
I fall between the tracks,
joining a nation in transit,
my breath slowly drifting away.

Do I Look Sexy in My Sari?

Blue mercurial eyes
porcelain white skin
freckles dotted across her face
peeping out from her carriage
you lay your hand across the railing
moulding her in your frame
the shutter release captures the moment
her translucent smile
shimmering in the background
at first blush you stand in front of her
adjusting your sari
two contours superimposed in celluloid
her childlike face oblivious to your intrusion
her frosted candour
crystalised in your reflection.

Star Struck

Ethereal and soft,
flowing lightly in the sky,
sequins of gold
speckled among the stars,
folds of satin
wrapped around
her delicate shape,
she reaches out,
holding onto
the thinly woven threads,
looped around her fingers,
carrying an unbroken promise,
radiant in the half-lit moon,
glimmers of hope,
shimmering in the faded colours,
ruffled edges severed
through a rush of teeming stars,
a galaxy of speckled dust
crumbling in her hands.

Ashoka

Without sorrow
I dissolve into
the bright orange petals
ready
to accept
your tears
ready
to open
my eyes
to your love.

Without sorrow
I am wilting
in the hot sun
your flesh
trembling
as I let go
and trample
on your love.

Without sorrow
I lie beaten
by the floral tributes
left on my grave.

Without sorrow
I let go
and stroll through
the empty parking lot
ready to accept
I am alone.

The Railway

Flies gather at my feet,
as I step across the tracks,
to wander among the empty carriages,
retracing the forgotten stories,
etched in these obsolete coaches,
their daily grind seeping into my skin,
unfinished journeys dwindle
in the evening sun,
empty carriages sterile and deserted,
their shadow shrivels
in the Monsoon rain,
fractured chains nailed to wall mounts,
broken links marooned in the past,
forgotten journeys to an outpost,
re-lived in glass cases,
flies gather at my feet,
as I wait in line,
for the train home.

Independence

They twist the strings
around their thin small arms,
on a busy junction,
paper kites tangled
in electric wires,
caught between the poles,
they dangle in the evening sun
huddled together
in this makeshift hamlet,
giggling against
the newly painted wall,
designed to keep them
off the road,
unravelling their kites
they nestle in between
the mounds of rubble
subsisting on scraps,
their humble homes
visible to the passing cars,
women in colourful saris
selling flags,
their husbands sharing stories
with their neighbours,
lounge
on an old corrugated steel roof,

oblivious to paper kites
gliding above their heads,
a carousel of pastel colours
spanning the skies.

The Fleadh

When you slide back the sheet
and leave behind your creased form
in the empty space
I lie in the loneliness of early morning,
adrift from the night we spent together,
our minds eclipsed in a wandering lust
of misplaced love,
I settle into the slow decline
of absent moments,
allowing the sun rays scratch away
the fragmented parts I can't recall,
and listen to the bin truck reversing up the hill,
your face withering in the morning air.

Kerala

Backwater creeks disappear,
landslides plunge through
God's country,
toppling homes,
their contents drifting
in the muddy water,
families trapped
in the heavy rains,
wading knee deep,
they watch
their future roll by,
debris swept along,
a river of tears
bleeding from their wounds,
clinging to rain-soaked branches,
brittle and bent over,
they cling on,
and watch
the backwater creeks
recede slowly,
wading knee deep
unbroken dreams.

The Lotus

You stand
on the threshold
of life,
buried deep underneath,
and wait for the sun
to rise from the east,
you begin to surface,
floating gracefully
flirting with the rays
shimmering above your head,
a tiny bud
seeking out the light
you open one petal at a time,
searching for the soft glow
travelling across your face,
in full bloom
your innocence eroded,
you bask in the radiant warmth
falling onto your skin,
you follow the sun
as it moves across the sky,
and settle in the evening flare,
you disappear beneath the surface,
as darkness closes in,
and end each day

sinking deeper and deeper
into the muddy pond
repeating the same cycle
each day,
you tread across this earth,
releasing hope along your journey,
and sit with legs crossed
and I watch you
waiver in the final blaze
each night.

Rain

Blurring
the fusion
of a city
in full bloom,
the mist
casts a shadow
on the handwoven
matrix
weaving through
the slums,
new buildings streaked
with rain,
casting doubt
over the unpolished
exterior of marbled walls,
our enthusiasm
fading
with every slippery step.

We can no longer see
the railway track,
as a dense fog
takes over,
we sit in the foyer
of the hotel,

watching the drops
being wiped away,
and wonder
when the mist will lift.

Black Clouds in Taj Mahal

Persian poems
inlaid with
jasper from the Punjab
reverberate
with thunder claps
rolling above
my head.

This porcelain marble dome
camouflaged in monotone greys
hanging low in the sky.

Sepia tones
linger in the rain,
a third wife
interred below.

A mirage
of a thousand elephants
carrying
white marble from Rajasthan
shimmers
in the reflecting pool.

Mundane stories
of mutilated hands
lurking in the shadows.

I watch them
sit on the bench
snapping poses
of loneliness and lost love,
trying to recreate
the lonely figure
who once sat here.

Her stillness
etched on these polished surfaces,
lifting my drenched face
toward the crescent moon,
I wallow
in the urban myths
seeping into this jewel,
leaving behind
the echoes of the past.

Stray Dogs

Thin razor-sharp dogs
prowl the neighbourhood,
stalking the streets,
in early morning,
lying in front of security huts,
they wait for the evening sun to set,
claiming territorial advantage
as dusk falls,
rummaging through all the rubbish,
they control the enclaves,
hidden behind shaded branches
and lie in wait in packs,
brave enough
to stand their ground
on those who stray
in their way.

Dragonflies

An empty space
the size of a ballroom
the scent of polished
marble floors
lingers in each room
ready to embrace
a new family
books stacked against
the window ledge
a carousel of dragonflies
hovering in mid-air
I sit by the window
and watch
the woman in her sari
taking away black bags of rubbish
gold bangles dangling from her wrist
the iron man pressing clothes
under a tree
I watch as layers of my life
peel away
and follow the bicycle
carrying boxes of candy
winding down the road
this is my new home
empty and full of promise

the laughter of children
echoing in another room
I watch the dragonflies
caught between the leafy branches
an arabesque pose
trapped in mid-air
I watch in silence
as they shimmer
in the midday sun
the monsoon
coming to an end
as I sit in my empty home
unburdened by the past.

Evening

I watch
a peacock
without feathers
tremble
in the evening light
traipse
across the well-worn
hotel lawn
and listen
to the faint hum
of life passing me by.

Waiting

Gold threads
frayed at the edges
silk wavering
in the blue light
a puff of smoke
blurring her face
she waits alone
in the darkened room
threadbare and barren
covering her bare shoulders
with her shawl
sequined mirrors shimmering
voices from the street
interrupt her reverie
inhaling the stale scent
drifting up from the pipes
she envelops the emptiness
seeping into the room
blurring her
mascara-stained cheeks
exhaling her bitter thoughts
night descends in a rush
erasing every fragment
of him, she waits alone
and listens to the trickle
of voices lingering below.

A Winter Morning in Delhi

The moon shimmers
in the speckled dust
of an early morning dew,
our scarves pulled
across our mouths
as we peer through
the heavy haze
of smoke drifting
through the branches,
a grey dawn
greets us as we
step out into this chilled air,
we smell the remnants
of burning embers,
smouldering in alley ways,
the auburn rays of the sun
trapped between
the charcoal sky,
we wait for it to rise,
and hope we can breathe again.

Paused

We seldom
find the time
to look into
each other's eyes
too busy
to stop
for one moment
and notice
the ever-changing hues.

We seldom
find time
to listen
to the brittle timbres
resonating
in our hearts
too busy
to stop the clock
for one moment
and feel the warmth
vibrating
from our bodies.

We seldom sit together
and watch
the sun rising

in the east
unable to unravel
the rays falling
towards the west.

Wrapped
in the glossy canopy
of modern life
where the virtual
dictates
how we spend our time
we forget
those early days
when we lounged around
and paused.

Today
we seldom
take time
to inhale
the ever-changing
blossoms
at our feet
as we fill our days
with endless moments
and forget to use
a full stop.

Masala Tea

Freshly brewed
tea leaves
a fusion of spices
steeped in the past
poured gently
into cracked delph
its delicate scent
lingers after
the pot is gone
and the embers
turn to ash.

Where Do We Go from Here?

Motorcycles swerving
onto the footpath,
tuk-tuks stalled
on zebra crossings,
cars in every direction
fly by,
trucks overtaking
on both sides,
horns beeping,
piercing
our eardrums,
we are stuck
between lanes
as large buses brush
against our skin,
exhaust fumes
tickling the hair
on the back of my legs,
bemused drivers
look on as we
contemplate where we go.

Only the Bones Remain

Grey ramshackled buildings,
Smashed panes of glass,
Broken wooden doors
Hanging from their hinges,
Dried blood splattered
On cracked walls.

Nothing is left
But the crumbling facade
Of a town where ordinary life
Has vanished,
Shells of cars covered in dust
Lie vacant in the street.

There is no one
To hold her hand,
No one to welcome her home,
As she stands in the doorway,
And smells the charred remains
Of a distant path.

**This poem was inspired by a story about a Syrian refugee who returned to her home in an abandoned ISIS controlled area and there was nothing left. The words she spoke "only the bones remain" have remained with me.*

Abandoned

The petals fell
like confetti
a hail of white
scattered
at her feet
she gathers up
her silk garment
and runs
through
the tunnel
leaving behind
a sprinkle of white dust
blowing lightly
in the autumn breeze
abandoning
her new family
she runs through
a maze of corridors
letting go
of the cold stares
emanating from the stone walls
she drifts
into the unknown
alone and relieved.

Dawn after Diwali

The muggy air
clings to my lungs,
wrapped around
each breath,
a blue flame
flickers
in early dawn,
plastic smoldering
down a laneway,
quilted figures
bent forward
warm tier hands,
the skyline
smudged in charcoal
a thick film of dust
settles on my skin
as I scurry along
the deserted streets,
a jaded sun
trying to break free,
a chill lingers
on the back of my neck,
forlorn branches
shaded in grey
shed their leaves,

a multi-coloured mask
shielding the smoke
drifting across my face,
I smell
the burnt-out crops
smoldering
above my head,
and follow the trail
of fallen leaves
scattered across the road,
each breath fading faster and faster.

There is No Moon Tonight

There is no moon
tonight
when I look
into your eyes
a cloudy haze
erases
your reflection
flickering above
the surface.

There is no moon
tonight
when we tremble
under the leafy branches
reaching deep
underneath your skin
we fall
into the unknown
and retrace
the lines etched
onto your face.

There is no moon
tonight
when we dance
to the unknown
heroes of our lives.

Tribal Echoes

The lights
shimmer through the trees
a slow crawl
of misplace youth
cradling their loneliness
on rooftop terraces.

They sway to the unknown beat
caught between the mangled notes,
and crackled voice
immersed in the sorrows
of old love songs,
thc flute tinged in a bittersweet
tale, fractured and broken,
they leave their hearts
in this place.

Their bodies torn
by the eyes hovering over them
unwanted and alone
they find a place
in a half-filled glass
cradling the essence
close to their heart,
invisible tears wiped away.

They walk in the shadow
we have created
and sway to the unknown beat,
the bodhrán rumbles over
their silent screams,
trapped in tradition,
they temper with this new song,
and dream of faraway fields.

Longing

I dream of you
sitting in the park
eyes closed
listening to the bustle
of our city passing
you by

I dream of you
seeking refuge
under leafy branches
from the Monsoon rain
your pashmina shielding
your face

I dream of you
as I sit alone
sipping a cold coffee
shrugging off
the nightshift far away

I dream of you
in your sari
and the day that
we can be together.

Elephant Ride

Majestic and tardy
they plod slowly along
eyes downcast
as they follow their master
the early-morning sun
beating down
as they carry their loads
cars weave through them
draped in sequins and
hand-painted jewels
they head towards the fort
majestic and tardy
carrying the weight
of all their memories
on every journey.

Diwali

Reaching out
to the soft glow
flickering

the light
falls
onto your face

a flame
in my heart
burning

our lips
touch and
I follow
the rays

tiptoeing
over
our hearts

our souls
burning

we embrace
the new light

shimmering
along the path

our lives
entwined
for another year.

A Toast

The Christmas tree
shimmers
in the darkness,
multi-coloured lights
flickering
through the night,
carols lingering in the air,
she stokes the last embers
and remembers the blue flame
reflected on his youthful face,
his voice filled the air
as he sang his favourite song,
toasting their love
each year
they draped their bodies in tinsel,
and glittered like falling stars,
swooning to all-time classics,
she remembers the curtains
being pulled, his song,
and then, it was over.

She watches the last blue flame,
withering in the cold night air,
the fairy-lights still shimmering
as she toasts their love
and remembers his voice
lingering in her heart.

Moti Bagh Traffic

Peacock feathers
with synthetic wings
in blue and green
shoved against
the window pane
families walking
between cars
street hawkers
tapping the window
with their wares
I turn away
and ignore
the scraping of the glass
at last she leaves
and I am free to
look out the window
and then I see
the scar on her face
as she steps beyond the traffic.

The Couple

Handsome
is not the word
I would use,
his lips pressed
against the starched white napkin,
wiping away the crumbs.

This was our first meeting,
and our only one
when we would be alone.

A Friday evening
we sat opposite each other,
peeling away
some of our layers,
I watched
the way his fingers
held the fork,
a delicate instrument
in his hands,
we fell into conversation.

Handsome
is not the word
I would use,

his ruffled hair
slipping over his eyes,
we touched our souls
in the falling light,
ready to entwine our lives forever.

Advent

Like a frantic butterfly
it shimmers erratically
a Christmas tree on fire
multi-coloured fairy lights
flickering candyfloss sugar highs
its pines coated with
snow-white needles
there is nothing left
when it's stripped bare
but the memories of another year gone.

Muffled Tones

Muffled voices
linger in the midnight air,
drifting along the marble staircase,
a car door slammed shut,
stilettos climbing the tiled steps,
limbs leaning against the railings,
words fudged
bodies brushing off the wall,
a siren screeching below,
the rattle of a key
dangling from the lock,
they stood in the doorway,
fumbling for the switch,
they stumble inside,
bottles opened, glasses clinked,
the strains of garbled voices
singing along to Leonard Cohen,
drifting up the marble staircase
as she lies awake
listening to the fading beat,
car lights flicker outside her room,
shadow dancing off the walls,
she dreams of silence,
through the muffled tones from below.

A Monsoon Lunch

Fork lightning
crackles
across the enclave
shrouded
in black thunder clouds
rolling off
the compounds,
the heavy rains
sapping up all our energies
we huddle under a tree
as the lights go out
the beeping *tuk-tuks*
disappearing down
hidden laneways
we hold onto our takeaways
waiting for the rain to pass.

A Christmas Lunch

We sit alone
underneath
the canopy
fairy-lights dangling
above our heads
waiters in gold Santa hats
a snow-covered tree
flashes in the corner
as we bathe
in the winter sun
Hindi music
seeps into our skin
the aromas of Delhi
filter through
and we sink deeper
and deeper
into this new world
leaving behind
the snow-covered paths
blending our traditions
into this new fusion
we sip an Irish coffee
in the winter sun
our feet tapping to a new beat.

The Window

The lace curtain
covers the soft hues
on her face
she peers through
the fine mesh
in the tiny latticed shutter
watching families bickering
on the street below
invisible and forgotten
her delicate features
bring her favours
locked in tradition
she smudges dark kohl
onto her moist eyelids
waiting to be selected
closed from the outside world
she slips back
unable to leave this maze
trembling in the morning dew
she returns to her room
hoping to be picked.

Tent City

Sitting on the edge
of the pink city
clusters of tents
wedged between
fairytale forts
a clothes line
shimmering
in burnt orange
a mother
with her child
strapped to her waist
peers in
on my white face
tapping the glass
with ornate nails
she commands me
to look into her soul
her voice penetrating
the window pane
I hear her pain
trapped among the gates
of this fortified city
buried deep in
ancient tales
festers in

the soft light
which descends
on this city
these faded pink walls
enticing me
to surrender
to the hushed voices
reverberating from
those speckled walls
and all I see
is a flame
a glimmer of hope
wavering behind
the underpass
burnt orange flickering
on the clothes and my soul
slowly shimmering
across the moonlit lake

Nothing Left Unsaid

It's the times we are apart
that we open up our hearts,
divulge our innermost secrets,
share a passing moment
in a different country,
my notifications alerting
me to every message,
watching pedestrians walking
passed my home on WhatsApp,
the brittle sun a reminder
of the cold short days of winter,
I delve into my old home life,
everyday,
cluttered bookshelves
of a life I have left behind.

I sit in a room with no books,
clean white walls freshly painted,
I embrace the sparseness
of my new existence,
the new memories which I have created
while we are apart,
I dwell on the frenzied pastiche
that lies in front of me,
and overload your inbox

with snaps and moments
you cannot share,
and it's while we are apart,
nothing is left unsaid.

New Beginnings

It's time to say goodbye
and listen to your heart
the papier-mâché stars shimmer
under a hail of fireworks
celebrating the end of another year
It's time to say goodbye
and see beyond the flickering
light glistening in the sky
shedding all the dead skin
from my body, in this place
I have flourished,
our parting is not the end
but a new beginning for me to grasp.

Grounded

It must have been
the death star I saw
on the way to the airport
a slight ripple on the Saturn moon
a small halo of light
shimmering through the dense fog
we sat on the runway
for hours, going nowhere.

I Am

What?
I am the stranger
You met in a bar
One night
I am the person
You brought home
After you kissed my hand.

What?
I am the lover
You cradled in your arms
On the single mattress
Your cotton sheet
Barely covering my exposed flesh.

What?
I am your friend
Sitting in an armchair
Listening to your stories
I am holding your hand
As we follow
An uncertain path.

What?
I am surrounded by lists
As we prepare to entwine
Parts of our souls together

I am full of resplendent thoughts
Disappearing
Before I walk down the aisle.

What?
I am the mother of two
Waiting for that bus to come
I am the mother of two
Who knows you will not come
I am the mother of two
Ready to leave
That uncertain path.

What?
I am waiting at the bus stop
Collecting the missing parts
I am walking away from you
And gathering the smiles
Left behind by our children.

What?
I am alone and happy
I am climbing trees
With our children
I am surrounded by teenage angst
And preschool pranks
But I am free
I am
I am me.

Selfie

In love
With yourself,
Self-indulgent
You gaze
Into the bitter lens
A lonely impulse
Airbrushed
From history
Your polished face
Drifting
In the virtual world,
You lean forward
Filling the frame,
Another starlet
Blazed
In a vacuum
Of millennial loss,
Your pixelated features
Forever blurred
Among the falling stars.

First Light

The first trickle of light
Peeping over the mountains
A warm brush with hope
Peels away the emptiness
Shrouded in the early mist
Grasping onto these tiny rays
I pull back the curtains
And watch a symphony of birds
Reclaim the dawn,
The sun glistening
On a carousel of flowers
Shedding its stars,
A ball of light rising above my head
I embrace this warm brush with hope
And glimpse Aurora traipsing
Across the waves,
A small flicker drifting
In the timbres of my heart.

Fastening the Sail

We linger longer
in the deep blue sea,
our fingers fastened
around our soulless night,
we capture favoured ones
as we slip between
the carousel of light
and linger longer
beneath the bow.

Bushfire

Memories
Crumpled in a flame
Discarded bric-a-brac
Sullied in the scorched earth
Vacant homes airbrushed
In subtle hues
Summer holidays
And new year plans
Dwindling in the endless heat
Monochrome news feeds of love ones
Trickle through
Disjointed and lost among the haze,
They pick through what's left behind
Retrieving faint echoes
From the embers that remain.

Remembrance

She tumbled down the steps
into the courtyard,
listening to children giggling outside,
their little feet pounded the pavement
playing hopscotch,
the sea whispered into her ears,
lost among this maze of graves
and headstones,
old baths in the corner
discarded over time,
she recalled the names
of old friends,
absent lives bathing
as children,
dark shadows spying,
grey shapes crawling across damp cold walls,
they sat on old wooden benches
facing the altar, their eyes consumed with fear,
she lit a candle in memory of their innocence.

Passer By

In time, standing to attention,
Missing the beats left behind,
A stolen loss wrapped
In yesterday's sorrow,
We collect the missing links
Etched onto our past,
Waiting for our souls
To fall in line
With the frayed threads
Dangling in the evening sun.

Meet Me at the Pier

Our days will never meet,
Our lives will never eclipse
Into the beautiful promise,
Your voice will never touch
Each timbre resonating in my soul,
Your music will never leave my heart,
When I linger at the pier,
Chasing your shadow among the stars.

Our days will never meet,
The warmth of your breath
Will never brush against my skin,
As I stand alone at the pier,
Waiting to see you among the stars.

Warbride

A child
Holding a bouquet,
Wilted leaves and petals
Falling onto her frock,
Gold bangles
Dangling in the cool air,
Her dark eyes
Dulled by too much kohl,
Dubbed in rouge
And coral lips
A mannequin ready to perform
She stands in the dust.

Her street empty
Of the sound of laughter,
Her building pockmarked
With the stains of war,
She walks towards her fate,
Taking his hand for the first time,
This child, drenched in fear.

What We Keep

(for Nisha Luthra)

Snapshots
held so tightly
unable
to release
the loss and hurt
bound up
in these faded images,
young faces
blemish free,
big eyes staring into the lens,
a lopsided smile
a sideways glance,
friends
holding tight
lost in the moment,
dreams and hopes
cascading through
silent lips
loyal to the end,
a creased print
pressed with
all the faded hues
seeping from our lives,
a patchwork
of our time

gathering dust,
a memory
locked
in the palm
of my hand.

Merchant With Cigarette

Sitting behind the counter
of this makeshift hut,
tattered newspaper print
holding the walls together,
old posters faded over time,
selling throat lozenges,
tobacco and coca cola
tied around the front,
dangling like the frayed
hem of a well-worn frock,
the merchant sits waiting each day,
lighting one cigarette after another,
the bare shelves behind him
covered in dust and
the grimes of war,
he sits in his hut, among the rubble,
unable to leave his post.

COVID 19

Find me
The crisp vapour dangling in mid-air,
Shrouded in yesterday's mistaken lull,
The sweet cube of your love
Dissolved in hazy solubles.

Find me
Among the broken vowels
Curled inward in your soul,
Our loss etched
In the shady groves
Waiting to be released.

Find me
Among the empty streets,
My lips subdued
In a sorrow I cannot escape.

Find me
Lying hunched over,
Dizzy with life,
Blending the voices in my head.

Find me
Lost in the cradle of your affection,

Entwined in the bitter
Fragments left behind.

Find me
A speck of dust,
With more.

Beyond Our Last Thoughts

Words streaming
in oblivion
lost among the grey surf,
sentences paused
in the slow ripples
cascading towards us,
our feet
drenched in the sultry tones
of real time,
bathed in grey,
we tinkle with each gush,
soaked in temptation
and an enduring stream
of mistaken cues,
the water receding from our toes,
we look beyond the horizon,
beyond our last thoughts.

My Life Before

Empty
missing the gentle gush
of your breath
on my skin,
our moist lips
sealed in a sloppy kiss,
we trail across
the vacant lines,
coloured
in a patchwork of green,
reclaiming the fragments
from our pebble dashed world,
we traverse across
the air miles,
overseeing the mottled pain
brewed in exile,
exploring the petty pangs
of yesterday's reel
fused in a tangled mesh
of the salted paradise
we left behind,
we wait in silence
undoing the knots
hoisted upon our shoulders.

My life before,
once empty,
once missing a beat.

My life before
clasped in the missing moments,
we pull the blinds down
and follow the trail.

Lemongrass and Ginger Tea

Six feet apart
I can still smell
your infused scent
wafting in the air
as we lingered
in the silence
of empty gazes
and masked faces.

Steam blurring
the moments we had together
before it was time to go
time to say goodbye
time to return without you
to a lockdown in another country
where I sit alone
by my window
sipping tea
and remember
the brief moment
we shared this summer.

This poem was previously published in Poetry in the Plague Year by Poetry Kit (2020/21).

Slots

Synchronised classes
With virtual friends
Unmuting the loneliness
Clasped in her hand,
She labours over forced strategies,
Composing and decomposing numbers
The trials of a seven-year-old
Condensed into the slots
One sided conversations, online,
Wrapped in a sugar-coated smile,
Her stilted voice paused,
Disconnected and detached
She fumbles over her lines,
A scratched recording
Drifting in and out,
She unmutes the emptiness
Inside her head,
And labours over a seesaw activity
an overload of virtual learning
In a world condensed
Into slots.

All is Going Well

Wilted basil delivered
To my door,
Overripe bananas
Soggy and bruised,
Indian pears crushed
In the palm of my hands.

I long to taste
Your soft lips
And bathe in your sweet scent,
No callers for fourteen days,
No going outside my door,
I wait in silence
Behind the blue sticker
Which marks me out.

Watching reruns of Delhi crime,
Scrolling through endless news feeds,
I wander around my empty home,
Branded and soiled,
Dreaming of when I can taste
The crushed pears upon your lips.

All is going well.

Sunrise

We have blended into dawn,
Faded into the orange glow,
Shapes wavering behind a screen,
A mirage of yesterday
Shimmering in the morning light,
Your white muslin kurta
Fraying at the edges
Blowing gently in the wind,
We blend into the sultry haze,
Our time singed with speckled rays,
Tinged in the warmth of your breath
We merge into the background,
Lost in the echoes of time,
Listlessly following the guide's voice
We tremble among the patterned mosaics,
Curved figures etched with patience,
A flowering lotus breathing life
Into the deadening heat,
We blend into the unknown
Unravelling the moments we were apart.

Taj Mahal

The echoes of your silence are lost,
Lost among the soft ripples
Gleaming from the tiny cracks
Which we can no longer see,
My body draped across the frosted marble,
Shimmering in an amber glow,
I look beyond the lens,
Beyond the emptiness of this vast tomb,
And cradle your memory in a snapshot,
The echoes of your silence
Seeping into my flesh,
Drifting into the emptiness,
You left behind,
You left behind your sorrow,
And bathed in a new light,
A future beyond this dome,
We re-create your sadness,
Your solitude and your solace,
As we stare beyond the cracks,
Grasping onto the shards of life,
Splintered across this vast tomb,
The echoes of your silence
Traipsing among our pain,
We leave behind a part of you,
Untarnished by the sun,
Lost in the vastness of this tomb.

This poem was previously published in Poetry in the Plague Year by Poetry Kit (2020/21).

Acknowledgements

I would like to thank all those who made this book possible — especially all the friends I met along the way while working at the Embassy of Ireland in New Delhi, playing darts in New Delhi, friends I met through the American Embassy School and all those I met along my way.

I would like to thank Nisha and Deepak Luthra who believed in me and always supported me.

About the Poet

Emer Davis was born in Ireland and has lived in London, Abu Dhabi and Delhi. She studied Communications and Film Studies in Dublin and currently works as a civil servant. She has been writing poetry and short stories for over 30 years and has been involved in various writers groups, including the Green Ink Irish Writers Group in London, Rooftop Rhythms in Abu Dhabi and Drogheda Creative Writers Group in Ireland. She set up the Poetry in the Park initiative in her local town in Ireland and organised the Drogheda Poetry Trail during the 2018 Fleadh.

Her work with the Syrian migrants on Lesvos island, Greece, with the European Migration Programme to support the resettlement of these refugees in the EU inspired her to write several poems about her experience there, which have been published widely. She was runner up of the 2018 Trocaire Poetry Ireland competition with her poem "Raqqa Bowl 2017". Several of her poems and stories have been published in Ireland, UK, Italy, Romania, UAE, USA, Nepal and India. Her poems have been translated into Irish, Italian and Romanian.

She has been living in India since 2018 and participated in the Chandigarh Literary Festival in 2020. More information about her poetry can be found on her webpage *bunnacurrypoet.org* .